WHAT I HAVE LEARNED FROM CHILDREN

WHAT I HAVE LEARNED FROM CHILDREN

Michaelene P. Grassli

Deseret Book Company
Salt Lake City, Utah

Photographs by Steve Bunderson

Library of Congress Cataloging-in-Publication Data
Grassli, Michaelene P., 1940–
    What I have learned from children / Michaelene P. Grassli.
       p. cm.
    ISBN 0-87579-701-6
    1. Children—Religious life. 2. Spiritual life—Church of Jesus
Christ of Latter-day Saints. 3. Church of Jesus Christ of Latter-
day Saints—Doctrines. 4. Mormon Church—Doctrines. 5. Grassli,
Michaelene P., 1940–   . I. Title.
BX8643.C56G73 1993
289.3'32'083—dc20   93-13328
                                                             CIP

Printed in the United States of America
10   9   8   7   6   5   4   3   2   1

CONTENTS

INTRODUCTION

One evening as we sat conversing with some dear friends around our fireplace, the question was raised, "What must we do to become as a little child?" This question piqued my interest. When the Savior appeared to the Nephites, some of his initial teachings instructed them to "become as a little child, or ye can in nowise inherit the kingdom of God." (3 Nephi 11:38.) When a concept is vital to our eternal salvation, it is given repeatedly in the scriptures and by the prophets. The counsel to become as a little child is so straightforward and appears so many times, it is evident that the Lord must be serious about it; therefore it bears considerable study and attention. If being childlike is what we have to do to be with him again, we need to understand what this means and learn how to accomplish it.

And so, at the suggestion of Ursula and Johann Wondra, our friends from Vienna, and with the encouragement of my husband, I have deliberated about what the Lord is trying to teach us when he says to become as a little child. This book is the result of those deliberations.

On the surface, this may seem to be a book about children directed exclusively to women. It is not. True, it is a book about children, but its message is for all adults who are trying to improve their lives. By examining the characteristics of children, we can learn what the Savior meant by holding them up as examples, and discover how we can refine and perfect ourselves by taking on some of these childlike qualities.

As I began exploring this topic, I first examined how I feel about children. I must warn you that my feelings may seem unrealistically enthusiastic to some. I recognize that and ask your indulgence, even your forgiveness, if you don't share those feelings. But keep reading anyway. Maybe my observations and ideas can enrich your feelings about and experience with children.

I think I was born loving children, and until I was nearly an adult I thought everyone else felt the same way. One of my earliest recollections is of loving babies and wanting to be with them. As the oldest cousin in both my mother's and father's families, and the oldest of six siblings, I had plenty of experience with children of all ages as I was growing up. My college major was home economics education, which included child development.

Children delight me! I ordered a dozen of them for my own. Nine of that dozen will have to be given to Leonard and me in the life to come, if we merit them. In the meantime, the three who were sent to us on this earth have been a source of wonder and joy and learning.

Jane Anne, Susan, and Sara are the three little girls, now grown, who solidified in me those tender feelings I had always had toward children. They taught me about being childlike and gave me opportunities to develop some childlike qualities.

Each of these three has established her own private territory in my heart. I acknowledge their individual contributions to the quality of my life, to my understanding of human nature, and to my devotion to children. Many of the stories that will follow in these pages are about my daughters, and I dedicate this book to them.

Someone once asked me which *age* of children is my favorite, and I have decided it is the age of the child in whose presence I happen to be. I think all children are fascinating. To me they are mysterious and lovable, as well as occasionally exasperating. My home and office are filled with their art and toys. I love to watch and to play their games. I am awed by their prayers. I love family home evening lessons taught by a five-year-old assisted by her three-year-old brother. I like the conversations children have when they don't know anyone is listening. I like their fascination with ladybugs, Heavenly Father, other children, and new experiences. I love their honesty, their tears, their jokes, and their hugs. I love their faith, their innocence, their humility, and their hope.

I am tickled to death with ten-year-old boys who try to gross me out with spiders, snakes, sneaky tricks, and vocabulary of blood and gore. I try to give them the reaction they want—you know, gasps and screams. And if I show genuine interest in the toad and am willing to hold the drippy snake innards, they think I am cool. Being in the presence of children, to me, is like being on holy ground, and when I am with them I feel overwhelming waves of love and tenderness.

I thoroughly enjoyed my motherhood years with our three daughters at home. I learned that, with children, the best things for a mother to do are often the hardest and take the most effort. Like changing dirty diapers. That's not much fun. Like getting out of bed in the morning and preparing a healthy breakfast. Like using placemats and setting the table. Like planning ahead for family home evening. Like thinking before speaking. Like exercising seemingly unending patience. Like cleaning things up even when you're tired. Like giving tough love. Almost nothing worth doing is very easy, and parenting certainly falls in that category.

I did get tired and I was challenged. But it was a satisfying tiredness, and the stimulation of learning more about children in general and about my children in particular outweighed the day-to-day worry and routine. Actually, my children kept my days from being routine. Many days I'd wake and think, "What new experience awaits me today?" And there was always something!

The joy repeats itself in my grandchildren, who at this writing number three. Some of the stories in this book are about Marie, Michael, and Marlies, who call me Grandma G. These little grandchildren are like dessert to me—they can be enjoyed openly and enthusiastically in all their sweetness. Already they are teaching me about spontaneity and devotion and faith. They lift my spirits, spice my life with joy, and generate in me great hope for the future.

With this background description of my feelings about children, let me turn now to what we can learn from them. The oft-repeated instructions for adults to *teach* children may obscure the importance of *learning from* them. But such learning would not only help us become more Christlike, it would in turn help the children to better love, trust, and follow us.

Learning from children requires first that we understand what they are like. Some characteristics of children are given in the scriptures. King Benjamin taught that children are "submissive, meek, humble, patient, full of love, willing to submit to all things." (Mosiah 3:19.) The Savior himself counseled, "Except ye be *converted,* and become as little children, ye shall not enter into the kingdom of heaven. Whosoever therefore shall *humble* himself as this little child, the same is greatest in the kingdom of heaven." (Matthew 18:3–4; italics added.) In addition, we are taught to "receive the kingdom of God as a little child." (Mark 10:15.)

In 3 Nephi 9:22, the Savior asks us to repent and come unto him as a little child, and we are told that "of such is the kingdom of God." If we repent, we approach the innocence of children. Children are unfettered by pride. They have simple faith and believing hearts. Adults tend to be more sophisticated and cynical; indeed, those who fail to become so are often labeled naive or foolish. In the context of the Lord's admonition, is being naive so bad? Is a believing heart something to criticize or ridicule?

A friend of mine said, "I've been trying to remember what I was like as a child. I keep thinking back about feelings I had then and I want to recapture them. Maybe that will help me 'become as a little child.' " I feel the same way. The more I observe children, the more I see in them and learn from them. They help me to remember what I was like as a child, and to know what I must do to regain or retain those childlike qualities.

In a popular movie fantasy, a twelve-year-old boy visiting

an amusement park wishes to be "big." His wish is granted. He wakes up the next morning with an adult body, but he is still twelve years old inside. The combination results in an engaging, appealing personality who, though vulnerable, endears himself to one and all. I suspect the writers of that film are like I am—a lover of children who thinks we should all recognize that children personify the best in mankind. This fantasy as it is played out on the movie screen gives us a glimpse of the possibilities of reality.

I do not believe the Lord means we should become like children in an unequivocal sense. I don't think he means us to be *childish*. Because of their limited experience, children tend to be selfish, impatient, and gullible. They often have poor judgment due to their lack of knowledge. I believe that kind of naivete is not what the Lord means when he asks us to be childlike. Such qualities as patience and wisdom and unselfishness usually come with maturity, and without them we act childishly.

When we are *childish*, we react to our Heavenly Father in spiritually immature ways. We get angry with him if things go wrong in our lives. We might decide to punish him with "temper tantrums"—that is, by refusing to obey the commandments, or to go to church, or to "be nice" to those who serve him.

Spiritually childish people are easily offended by or critical of Church leaders. To be spiritually childish is to "stop believing" because it seems easier to reject the lawgiver than to follow the law, to face our mistakes and correct them. Our refusal to believe makes us comfortable with our mistakes, a condition that leads to that unfeeling state described by Nephi in connection with Laman and Lemuel. (See 1 Nephi 17:45.) The thesis of this book is that in our maturity, we need to continue to cultivate the best qualities of children, the Christlike qualities that actually lead us to greater spiritual maturity.

Betty Jo Jepsen, first counselor in the Primary general presidency, has said, "Children are a gentle reminder of our divine beginnings and a model for our immortality." In the chapters that follow, I have tried to explore the qualities of children that I believe can remind us of our divine beginnings and regenerate the children within us world-weary, cynical grown-ups. Understanding children is a key to understanding ourselves. The child inside can draw us to our heavenly home. Entire books have been written about each of these qualities, and others as well, by those whose insight and wisdom far exceed mine. I have attempted simply to record my own observations of children and adults who exemplify childlike qualities, and to reflect on how they can be models for our immortality. The stories are true. Where sensitivity requires it, some names have been changed.

This book isn't intended to be a treatise on child development, but I have made some generalizations that for the most part represent children, and may help you understand better the children you know. Please don't get sidetracked if what is written here doesn't apply in every way to every child. I realize each child is unique.

I hope you will be drawn as I have been to children, that you will want to understand them, be with them, love them, nurture them, protect them, and, most of all, be like them. I believe such desires will help us be more worthy to be in the presence of our Father and our Savior.

Chapter One

A CHILD IS INNOCENT

*"Every spirit of man was innocent in the beginning;
and God having redeemed man from the fall, men became again,
in their infant state, innocent before God."*
(D&C 93:38.)

F our-year-old Sherrie had been lost for some time. When after much searching she was found, her father gently chided her, saying, "Honey, little girls must always tell their daddies where they are going."

Sherrie looked up at her father with wide-eyed innocence and said, "But Daddy, sometimes little girls don't *know* where they are going!"

Sherrie's response to her father expresses the condition in which little spirits come into this world—without information and without experience. They don't know who they are or where they're going. Someone has to tell them. And because of the gift of Jesus' atonement, they are also free from sin, or in a state of innocence. "Little children are whole, for they are not capable of committing sin." (Moroni 8:8.) They are untainted and pure. They are "alive in Christ." (Moroni 8:12.) As they grow, unless their normal development is impaired or deficient, they gradually become accountable. At age eight a child is baptized, formalizing and acknowledging this accountability.

The Lord says to repent and become as a little child. Does that mean we should repent and become free from sin? Because of our mortality we are imperfect. But through the blood of Christ we can become innocent, after all we can do. It is imperative that we see the good from the evil in order to be able to choose and fulfill one of the purposes of earth life.

The innocence of children is evident in daily experiences. Sometimes it makes for pretty humorous conversations. Becky and Sarah were excited about changing their Primary classes the first week in January. They wanted to know which classes they'd be in. Their mother explained, "Sarah, last year you were in the Nursery. Now you'll be a Sunbeam. And Becky, you were a Sunbeam, and now you'll be a Star."

A Child Is Innocent

Becky grinned as her mother continued, "And after you're a Star you'll be . . . "

"I know, I know!" she broke in. "Next I'll be a—, a—, I'll be a—VCR!"

My neighbor told me that her three-year-old Emily's favorite song is "Little Purple Panties." Maybe Emily knows panties better than pansies.

Four-year-old Michael asked his friend as they were playing, "Will you miss me when I go on my mission?"

The friend's mother was nearby and had overheard. "Are you going on a mission, Michael?" she asked.

"Yep!"

"Won't you miss your Mommy and Daddy?"

"Oh," he replied confidently, "they're going with me."

Of course, the innocence required of us is different from the simple lack of information or experience illustrated in these stories. It is *purity* that the Lord wants. Although they can be mischievous, children have that purity.

After baptism children are still innocent of many things. Eight-year-old Shelley couldn't go to sleep. She tossed and turned in worry and guilt. Finally she called her mother to her bedroom. "Mom, I can't sleep," she complained.

"What's the matter, dear?"

It took several attempts before Shelley could get the words out. "When we were playing outside today, some big boys made Mary and me pull down our pants."

Because Shelley was innocent, she was deeply troubled by what had taken place. Her mother helped her understand that the incident was not her fault, and that she was not a bad girl. With that reassurance, Shelley was able to go to sleep.

If we are to become as little children, we too must be troubled by evil. The world would rob us of our innocence, but cannot do so without our consent. We can choose to remain innocent of vulgar language, immoral acts, dishonesty, and lawlessness. We can choose to reverence the Sabbath, honor our parents, and love our neighbors.

"If there is anything virtuous, lovely, or of good report or praiseworthy, we seek after these things." (Article of Faith 13.) These poetic words of the Prophet Joseph Smith could help us establish a standard as we seek for innocence. The prophet Mormon gives another great test for judging an experience: "Every thing which inviteth to do good, and to persuade to believe in Christ, is sent forth by the power and gift of Christ; wherefore ye may know with a perfect knowledge it is of God." (Moroni 7:16.) If we are to become as little children, we will energetically resist evil that draws us away from Christ and robs us of our innocence. Television, movies, literature, music, places, and people that are not lovely or of good report or praiseworthy can't be part of our lives.

The innocence of children also allows them to be fully and enthusiastically involved in every minute of their lives. Elder James M. Paramore has said:

"They seek new experiences, they have no pretense or scorn or condescension or pride. They are natural and warm and outgoing. They are excited about the smallest things, and as such, captivate our attention. They experience each day with newness, not building upon the difficulties of the previous day. They don't even remember them. They teach us that spontaneity and excitement for life are essential to happiness and self-fulfillment, and really come from a loving God. . . .

"They are anxiously engaged and enthusiastic. . . . Each day is a wonderful, new, expanding experience, unencumbered by the previous day's issues or troubles. Those troubles are forgotten, and new opportunities and joy and living are again theirs. The vitality of their lives in these things is a wonder to behold. If we can retain this great power, how blessed will be the days of our lives and all those who are around us!" ("Become as a Little Child," *Brigham Young University 1982–83 Fireside and Devotional Speeches* [May 8, 1983], p. 123.)

Knowing the possible pitfalls of a given direction may cause us to avoid progressing in that or any path. Innocent enthusiasm moves us beyond merely wishing to taking action. It is a driving force behind accomplishment. Enthusiasm is a catalyzing ingredient in temporal and spiritual progress.

One truly magnificent reality of our imperfect and sometimes painful mortal existence is that every day—every minute—is a new, blank page of life. Regardless of our past, we can have a fresh start at any moment and write on that page what we choose. We are empowered in that by the Savior, in whom all becomes new. We are limited only by our own degree of desire, resolve, or commitment. Circumstances may seem to limit us, but circumstances are only incidental to people determined to succeed.

If you are passed over for a promotion at work, how will you respond? Will you criticize the one who was promoted or the judgment of the supervisor? Or will you congratulate your co-worker and be so gracious and conscientious that the supervisor recognizes your true worth and appreciates your excellent qualities? Will you let the actions of your supervisor determine how you will behave, or will *you* choose?

Some adults who show qualities of innocence can be deceived because of their trusting hearts. However, adults who are trying to maintain or regain innocence have an advantage over children because they have more experience and can process information better. Decisions need to be made on the basis not only of trust, but also of adequate information. This way, trusting, innocent people can avoid being victimized by the unscrupulous.

This brings to my mind, also, the need for us never to put another in the position of being victimized in any way. Physical, emotional, or financial victimization of others to any degree will rob us of our innocence and of earthly and eternal blessings. When we treat each other fairly, we preserve our own innocence and that of the people with whom we deal.

The beauty of innocence is that it can be recaptured when it is lost. If we have lived unworthily in some regard, we need not continue. We can put it behind us with repentance and forgiveness. Some mistakes are harder to resolve than others, but it can be done. Each day is a chance to start anew.

One common roadblock to reclaiming innocence through repentance is the inability we often have to forgive ourselves of past wrongdoing. We carry some burdens unnecessarily, and they weigh on us and affect our relationships.

Children are inclined to forgive themselves and others easily. Notice next time you see children having a disagreement. Minutes later they'll be reconciled. A child will be momentarily distraught over having spilled a glass of milk, but once it's cleaned up, if the child is reassured, he or she can resume eating or playing, having forgotten the mishap. If children can do this, surely we adults of vision and purpose can forgive ourselves when repentance and forgiveness have taken place.

We can become children in Christ, innocent and pure. Let us hold fast to our innocence where it exists, and reclaim innocence where we can, to draw ourselves closer to the childlike condition we seek. Let us choose to live each day free from activities and decisions that would rob us of our innocence. Let us choose for ourselves how we will respond to daily circumstances. Let us develop the innocence of children.

Chapter Two

A CHILD IS BELIEVING

"For God so loved the world,
that he gave his only begotten Son,
that whosoever believeth in him should not perish,
but have everlasting life."
(John 3:16.)

My friend Jan, substituting in her son's Primary class, was teaching a lesson about faith. As Jan explained that we haven't seen Heavenly Father, but we believe in him and have faith in his existence, she noticed quizzical looks on the faces of the children in the class.

Finally Kara raised her hand and said, "But Sister Blackburn, we *have* seen Heavenly Father." Jan was taken aback momentarily. Kara added, "We lived with him once. Of course, we've seen him!" There was no question in Kara's pure child heart and mind. She believed. And she was right, of course.

Children have believing hearts. They come into this world with the need for physical nourishment and security. These have been identified as the most driving needs of infants and toddlers. The fulfillment of these early needs generates in children trust and the ability to believe. Then we can help put into their mortal minds what their spirits knew before they came here. We can help them gain spiritual security. We can help them retain their believing hearts.

Four-year-old Michael was playing at a friend's home. His eighteen-month-old sister, Marlies, was there too, and, as eighteen-month-olds often do, she had grabbed and bothered until Michael's patience was sorely tested. At lunch, as Michael offered the blessing, he interjected, "Heavenly Father, please take Marlies for just a little while so she won't ruin our Lego setup."

Heavenly Father could do anything. Surely he could just "tend" the baby and keep her out of the way temporarily.

Children, especially young ones, understand the world in very literal terms. When four-year-old Amelia's mother and father were talking about a family wedding, Amelia asked, "What is 'falling in love'? Can you get up again?"

That kind of literal understanding makes it easy for children to perceive Heavenly Father as a reality, particularly if the children know and can trust their earthly fathers. It is easy to believe in Jesus when he is identified as someone who cares, and who has exhibited love for all of us. Children without fathers need to be exposed to good and righteous men who can become earthly manifestations of their Heavenly Father. As a result of that good example, children will be more likely to believe what trusted adults tell them.

Jan and her husband adopted a baby. When four-year-old Scott, a neighbor, came to visit, he looked at Jan, scrutinizing her carefully. Then he looked at the baby. Curious, he asked, "How did that baby get here? You didn't have a big tummy. Where did she come from?"

Not wanting to go into too much detail, Jan replied,

"You're right, Scott. This baby didn't grow inside me, but Heavenly Father brought her just the same."

Scott's eyes got big in amazement. He sputtered, "You mean . . . you mean he was *right here* and you didn't call me!"

Not only do children find it easy to believe, they also have a hunger to know *what* to believe. They usually want all the information they can get. Scott wanted to be there if Heavenly Father came.

It is fortunate that we begin life believing; that's a good place to start! As we grow and are exposed to the realities of life, we become more and more discerning. Then our spiritual and mental development allows us to understand and make judgments and choices. But if, in this maturing process, we can increase in wisdom while retaining that believing heart of childhood, we approach the childlike state spoken of by the Savior.

It is not enough to believe simply in the existence of Deity. We also need to know the capacity of the Godhead to have an effect on our personal mortal and postmortal lives. Children have the ability to believe in that power.

Nine-year-old Brittany told in sacrament meeting an experience that demonstrated her believing heart: "When I was five years old, my mom received a phone call that really upset her.

Dad had been electrocuted by a power line with 7,200 volts; then as he was lying on the ground his legs were run over by a pickup. I was really scared so I went up to my room, knelt by my bed, and prayed. I asked Heavenly Father to help my dad feel better and that he would be okay. When I got up, I felt good inside because I knew he would be all right. I wasn't afraid anymore. My mom brought my dad home later, and although he couldn't walk for a while, he had no broken bones and no burns. I wasn't surprised because Heavenly Father had told me he would be okay."

The fact that Brittany's father lived may not be particularly relevant to the feeling she had. Even if he had died she could have been comforted, knowing he was "okay." Her belief enabled her to feel the comfort given to her by her Heavenly Father.

Although we go through periods of believing, most of us also experience periods of some degree of doubt. In those instances, when we desire to believe but find faith faltering, if we will continue in our desire and in patiently praying, walking through each day doing the necessary and good, we will find belief growing stronger. If we are watching for it, we can see a phrase, a word, a lesson, a paragraph, a comment, or an experience shared by someone that will increase our faith and belief.

But the *desire* to believe is a critical component, because it demonstrates our willingness to put ourselves in the hands of our Father, to turn ourselves over to him and to trust in him.

Seven-year-old Eric and his family were being taught by the missionaries. After hearing about the Book of Mormon, Eric asked, "How can we know if it's true?" The missionaries asked him what he thought he could do to find out. "I guess I could ask God, and he'd tell me," came the response. At that point, the missionaries committed each member of the family to pray and ask God if the book were true.

As they finished the discussion, the missionaries asked if they could say a closing prayer. Little Eric said, "Why don't we pray right now to find out if the Book of Mormon is true?" And then he offered a simple prayer: "God, I want to thank you for the things we talked about. I'm excited about it, and I just want to know, is the Book of Mormon true?" Here there was a pause and the Spirit flooded in upon the little family. Then Eric continued, "I sure hope so because I feel really good inside." He had a desire to know. He had a desire to believe.

After the prayer, the missionaries invited all the family members to explain how they had felt during the prayer. They helped the family recognize that the Holy Ghost had witnessed to them that the answer Eric had prayed for had indeed been given to them.

Another way to develop a believing heart is to remember the believing heart you had as a child. One day Stephanie was riding in the car with her parents. She began to express some confusion over testimony. "I don't know if I have a testimony," she said. "I really don't know if the Church is true or not."

Her mother wisely replied: "A testimony is a good thing to wonder about, because it is a personal thing—only you can know what you believe. But let me help you remember some things that I think you might not know are part of your testimony. Do you remember when you and Eliza were talking about a lesson you had in Primary and you said it made both of you feel happy inside to talk about things you learned at Church?

"Another time we were in sacrament meeting and the speaker was telling us about prayer. He said that Heavenly Father hears our prayers and answers them. You turned to me and said, 'I know that too.'

"And then, one morning after we finished reading scriptures and had family prayer, you kept your scriptures open and reread the passages we had studied. I asked you what you were reading and you said, 'I feel warm inside when I read the scriptures.'

"Stephanie, each one of those experiences was the Spirit telling or confirming to you that the gospel of Jesus Christ is true."

Stephanie responded, "I guess I do have a testimony!" Then with excitement she related other experiences where she had received a confirmation of the Spirit.

I have reread some of my own journal entries and college papers that express how I felt in earlier years. This has been a great strengthening influence on me. I believe that spending some time in reflection on our childhood feelings is worthwhile.

Susan, age five, suffered from frequent nightmares. Full of faith, she asked her daddy to bless her that she wouldn't have bad dreams. He did bless her and her nightmares ceased. In her adult years, if she finds faith faltering, perhaps remembering that occasion will help.

Young adults sometimes have a tendency to lose heart or to lose faith as they increase in experience. One young man felt that his prayers had not been answered at a time when he needed help desperately. He confided to his father that he would never be the same again. He felt he would never be the

sweet and believing person that he had been as a youngster.

Sadly, he had become cynical in his attitudes about the Church as well as in his relationships with other people.

It is true that we are never the same as we were in childhood. When we have challenging experiences, our understanding of life and living increases and becomes deep and meaningful. But we can have that understanding and still maintain our testimonies and our believing hearts.

When our intellect expands, it sometimes overrules our faith and inspiration. What a sad loss! Our intellect should *serve* our faith and enlighten it.

Little Ulrike lay dying in the hospital. However, a priesthood blessing assured her parents that she would recover. The doctors performed an operation, but told the parents it was unsuccessful, and that there was no hope Ulrike would survive. The parents struggled with these conflicting conclusions. The judgment of medical science seemed to outweigh the priesthood promises.

Children would likely not find such conflict between faith and intellect. It is easy for them to believe that all things are possible.

Driving home from the hospital, the distraught parents heard President David O. McKay give his last powerful testimony of the Savior in a broadcast of general conference. President McKay spoke of the raising of Lazarus from the dead, and it seemed he spoke directly to the hearts of these loving parents. They were able to overcome their doubts and set their whole faith and confidence in the Lord and his priesthood.

Ulrike is today a healthy, grown woman.

A father gave his son a blessing prior to the son's departure for a mission. In the blessing, the father was prompted to promise the boy he would have dozens of baptisms. Afterward, logic took over and the father thought, "Why did I do that? Missionaries in that mission are lucky to have one baptism in their entire term of service. I am just a wishful father!"

What this father could not know was that a few months after his son entered the mission field in Germany, the barriers separating east and west would fall. This young missionary would then be sent into the eastern part of Germany, where many were waiting for the gospel.

The father followed the prompting of the Spirit, but his intellect nearly took over. To give our intellect dominion over our inspiration is a sure way to lose that inspiration. If we want to become as little children, we can learn from them to follow our feelings, not questioning our faith.

In faithful Saints around the world, I see enormously believing hearts. Sacrifices are common. A family in Bolivia will take turns attending church because family income won't allow them all to travel on public transportation. Besides, if there's nobody home, their property may be stolen or vandalized.

A faithful man and his wife both left secure employment in France to preside over a mission in Italy. In addition, they relinquished their apartment and would be on a long waiting list to acquire another one upon their return. Yet the glow of their believing hearts has carried them forward in the work to which they are totally dedicated, trusting that the Lord will provide.

Our General Authorities have been gathered out of many lands. They sell their homes and their businesses; they leave their native lands, some permanently. They accept the calls that come, knowing in some cases that they will be separated from loved ones, and that their income will be dramatically reduced. Yet their believing hearts make these sacrifices possible.

Children can believe because they are humble and teachable. They want to believe, they ask what to believe and how to believe, then they move on, believing.

To become as little children, we can follow this example and cultivate our own believing hearts.

Chapter Three

A CHILD IS HUMBLE

"Whosoever therefore shall humble himself
as this little child, the same is greatest
in the kingdom of heaven."
(Matthew 18:4.)

W e watched our granddaughter Marie as she was playing in a swimming pool with Krystal, a new friend. Both six-year-olds were reveling in the warm water. They tried to outdo each other in holding their breath under water, floating on their backs, and swimming the farthest. They were nearly equal in ability, and both seemed to enjoy the competition and the play. The time for swimming drew to a close and we called for the girls to get out of the pool. Marie looked at Krystal and said, "Let's have one more chicken fight! Can we, Grandma G?" she pleaded. I agreed, and off they went to the other end of the pool.

I hadn't been paying much attention to the girls' earlier play, so I watched with interest to see what a chicken fight was. Apparently a chicken fight is when two people hang by their hands on either side of the diving board at the same time. The object is to push the other person with your feet until he or she can no longer hold on to the diving board, and falls into the water. As the girls pushed and shoved and laughed and giggled, I could see again that they were very evenly matched. Marie would give a couple of good pushes to Krystal's midsection, and Krystal would push back. Krystal's legs closed around Marie's waist and Marie wriggled and stretched until she was free. I was surprised at how long they kept it up. As

Marie gave a particularly hard push with her foot into Krystal's belly, it looked to me as though it might have hurt Krystal. Immediately Marie released her hands, fell into the water, and said, "You win, you win!"

While that might be a lesson on kindness, to me it was also a demonstration of humility. Marie did not have to win. She subjected her competitive spirit and potential pride to a higher principle.

Marie's mother, Jane Anne, was the same way. At about age nine, when many girls are becoming cliquish, I anticipated Jane Anne might also experience that phase. In fact, I worried *for* her if she wasn't included somewhere. But she said, in all her nine-year-old wisdom, "Mom, some girls get mad if their friend plays with somebody else. But I know Diane likes me, and if she plays with someone else, I know she won't care if I do that too."

Is it pride that makes us critical, possessive, or jealous of each other? Humility enables us to truly rejoice at others' successes and mourn with them through trouble.

Little Mindy, sitting next to her mother in an Easter program in sacrament meeting, heard the words, "Jesus had died." She turned to her mother and in the stage whisper of a three-year-old said, "Jesus died?" Her mother nodded. Mindy repeated, "He did? Why didn't you tell me about it?" Mindy is teachable. She wants to know. Is this desire for truth and knowledge what the Savior meant when he said we should be humble? Maybe that's part of it.

Children want to know the truth. Four-year-old Robbie asked his mother if there was really a Santa Claus. His mother, not wanting to ruin Christmas for her little boy, yet not wanting to compromise the truth, said, "Well, when Jesus was born they gave him gifts, and we like to give gifts to each other, and Santa Claus is sort of the spirit of that gift giving."

Robbie listened intently. His mother went on, "Santa Claus is sort of in everybody's heart. We like to think about Santa when we give each other gifts. It's fun to sing songs about Santa. Santa Claus is one of the fun things about Christmas."

Robbie, with his eyebrows furrowed, said to his mother, "Mama, I'm going to ask you the question again, and this time I just want you to answer yes or no. Is there a Santa?"

"No, honey, there isn't."

"That's what I thought," he said, and went happily off to play. Children want to know the truth, and they accept it.

Connie and her younger sister, Susen, played frequently in our backyard. One day, I could hear their conversations through the open kitchen window. I think that day Susen must have been tired or perhaps not feeling well. Ordinarily she was not a cranky child, but this day she wanted Connie to push her on the swing. She wanted to have Connie help her with the dress-ups. She fussed when Connie started to get on her bike and leave the yard. Connie came back. Connie and her friends started to climb the tree. Susen fussed to come up with them. Connie lifted her up. I expected Connie to get angry, and I marveled at her patience with her little sister. Although Connie was not a pushover, she carefully helped her little sister. Responding to every demand, she was not easily stirred to anger.

Children, being the youngest members of society, also have the least status. Jesus was born in lowly circumstances. Does that mean that lowliness is acceptable? Perhaps some of the most lowly of Saints are most worthy of spiritual blessings.

Some of the fruits of accepting the gospel often include rising from poverty and deprivation. With those blessings comes increased accountability for our temporal stewardship. I believe that in humility we find an increased ability for the modest and wise use of our resources. Most little children do not seek for more and more material possessions, except as they are exposed to the influence of their peers and to the propaganda of television commercials. Usually they are pleased with modest acquisitions unless adults condition them otherwise. Is this what the Savior meant by being humble as a little child? Maybe that's part of it.

I have been inspired by the life-style of my parents. As a physician, my father had an above-average income. However, while my parents haven't wanted for anything, they have been modest in their spending. They don't have the fanciest home or the most expensive cars and clothes. Missions (they have served four) and education have taken the highest priority in their long-range plans. I believe that to be a demonstration of humility.

Humility is so necessary that our Father allowed us mortal weaknesses to overcome. "And if men come unto me I will show unto them their weakness. I give unto men weakness that they may be humble; and my grace is sufficient for all men that humble themselves before me; for if they humble themselves before me, and have faith in me, then will I make weak things become strong unto them." (Ether 12:27.) Our Heavenly Father in his wisdom blessed us with opportunities to rid ourselves of the great sin of pride. As we do so, his grace can turn our very weaknesses into our strengths.

I used to think of humility in a negative sense that sometimes made me depressed, but I have come to understand it in a different light. To me now, humility is admitting your weaknesses without concluding that you are inferior. Humility is recognizing your limitations and even your failures, but not concluding that you are a failure. Humility is knowing that you sin—and feeling sorrow for those sins—but not writing yourself off as being hopeless or unworthy of God's help and love. Humble people are in awe of the greatness of God, but this awe does not make them feel unimportant as individuals.

Humility is not the same as beating ourselves into the ground. We can have humility and confidence at the same time. If we come humbly to Christ, recognizing our dependence on him, we are prepared to be taught. Then our increased knowledge gives us confidence.

One of the finest examples of humility, I think, is Ammon, the son of Mosiah. He set out to preach the gospel to the Lamanites. He found favor in the sight of King Lamoni but declined marriage to the king's daughter—a marriage that would have put him immediately in a position of power as a member of the king's family. He asked only to be a servant to the king. Ammon said, "I know that I am nothing; as to my strength I am weak." (Alma 26:12.)

Can you imagine this statement from a man who, with great physical and spiritual strength, singlehandedly protected King Lamoni's flocks from raiders, converted the king and many of his people, established a church, rescued his brothers from prison, and led the people in righteousness? All that, and Ammon said, "I know that I am nothing; as to my strength I am weak"! His humility came as he recognized that his strength was from the Lord.

Our prophets have taught us to be humble. President Ezra Taft Benson has said, "God will have a humble people. Either we can choose to be humble or we can be compelled to be humble." (*Ensign*, May 1989, p. 6.) Recognizing that the Lord is the source of our blessings is an elementary step in achieving true humility.

I believe this true humility stimulates ever-spiraling upward progress. It does not deter us from reaching our potential, as false humility often does. For example, I visited in a stake where members of a new stake presidency were obviously uncomfortable with their new positions of responsibility. After a year of serving they had still not overcome their initial normal feelings of inadequacy. At this point, the members of their stake needed to see a presidency who, while humble, had backbone and vision. Their stake needed leaders, and the so-called humility of this presidency was debilitating to them. In our humility, we must move forward knowing that the Lord wants us to succeed and will imbue us with the qualities we need.

In the Primary general office, when a member of our staff or presidency has a birthday, I always ask her to share with us her philosophy of life. One of our staff members responded that she believes it is important to make decisions and then to move forward once the decision is made without continuing to deliberate on whether the decision was right. She said she has learned to assume that a decision is right and then to work to make it so.

To me, that philosophy exemplifies a facet of humility. I think the Lord intended that we not waste time in needless regret, but that we get on with our lives. Otherwise we are unable to experience the joy with which he is so willing to bless us. While the natural humility of children is a gift to them, we grown-ups usually have to cultivate true, appropriate humility. We can do that by sometimes subjecting a competitive spirit, as Marie did. We can bridle jealous pride, as Jane Anne did. We can be teachable, as Mindy was. We can be not easily stirred to anger, as Connie showed us. We can use our resources wisely, as my parents have seemed to do. We can accept truth, as Robbie did. We can balance humility with confidence, as Ammon did. This humility, so readily shown by children, can be ours, too.

Chapter Four

A CHILD IS LOVING

"Beloved, let us love one another: for love is of God;
and every one that loveth is born of God,
and knoweth God."
(1 John 4:7.)

J anie bounced in the door after school one afternoon. "Mom!" she shouted. "Mom, there is a new girl in school and we are going to be such good friends."

"Tell me about her, honey," her mom replied.

"She is so nice to me and she knows how to do a lot of things. She's really good at four-square and she makes everybody laugh. Her name is Cynthia and everybody likes her."

Day after day Janie reported the latest adventures at school with Cynthia, excited about the new friend she had found. One day with her mother's permission she brought Cynthia home after school to play.

Cynthia was black. Janie was not. In fact, Cynthia was the only black child in the school, and the first black child Janie had ever known personally. But Janie had not once mentioned to her mother that Cynthia was different from her in any way. It simply wasn't an issue for her. Her mother, pleased at Janie's ability to accept others, encouraged the little girls' friendship.

The world is in great need of the kind of unrestrained love that children give so naturally.

One Sunday morning, I attended a small Primary in Japan. A beautiful child of about six was intensely interested in this strange-looking visitor. Her affections for me, a total stranger, shone in her sweet little face. I could see her love and trust for everyone around her: teachers, parents, friends, and leaders. She glowed with such a pure and uninhibited love, so unrestrained and without self-consciousness, that I wanted to keep hugging her. How we adults need to be able to give that kind of open affection unconditionally!

As a Down's syndrome child, seven-year-old Andre had not had companions his age. His mother wanted him to be in a regular school so that he could have some friends to play with. The first-grade teachers prepared the class before Andre came the first day. They explained that he would need some help, that he needed friends, and that the children should be nice to him. The teachers thought it might be a good idea to assign buddies to Andre on a rotation basis so there would always be someone specific who could help him.

In the beginning the children wanted to "mother" Andre. They were so helpful that the buddy system wasn't necessary. The teachers even had to remind them that Andre needed to learn to do things for himself. As the year progressed, Andre did learn, and soon it was the children who were reminding the teachers that he could do things for himself.

In a March parent-teacher conference that year, Andre's mother wept in gratitude. She reported to his teacher that Andre had had his first invitation to a birthday party, and that another child had actually invited him to stay overnight at his house. The unconditional love of those children was beyond what the teachers and parents had even hoped for.

Bobby, a six-year-old boy with a disfigured face, visited in a Primary class taught by a friend of mine. He came in and sat, body trembling, in the opening exercises. In class, the teacher introduced the frightened little boy by name to the regular members of the class and then asked Lynda to give the prayer. In the prayer Lynda, unprompted, thanked Heavenly Father that Bobby could be in Primary with them that day. Following the prayer the teacher noticed that Bobby was no longer trembling, that he sat a little straighter, that he seemed not to be frightened. He participated in the class, although he suffered from a severe speech impediment. Lynda's tender, sensitive prayer had brought an unusually strong spirit into the class that day. After Primary, the little boy hugged the teacher and said, "Oh, I like this Primary best of all."

The teacher, reflecting on the incident, said, "These children inspire me with their unconditional love. They teach me every Sunday. I have been shown heaven and my testimony has been strengthened by these mighty little spirits."

Because children are so impressionable, they are easy prey to the prejudice of others. In their desire to imitate adults, they tend to adopt the opinions of adults close to them. As we rid ourselves of prejudice and bigotry, we will be less likely to rob children of their unconditional love, and we too will become more childlike.

Because of their ability to love unconditionally, children also often fall victim to abuse. Their judgment is generally limited by their lack of experience, and because they have been taught to obey adults, they may not be able to discern when an adult instructs them inappropriately. This is one case when the natural inclination for unconditional love could turn out to be a handicap for a child. We grown-ups must protect our children from abuse, in case they are unable to discern.

I am amazed at the natural sensitivities of children and their abilities to love. Susan, Julie, Ryan, and Johnny, cousins from two families, went with their grandmother to a children's museum. As the children watched a fifteen-minute film, the grandmother observed that the two little boys were wiggling in their seats and pushing each other playfully. Understanding that playfulness is characteristic of six-year-olds, and observing that they weren't really bothering anyone, she stood by and watched in amusement.

Soon she noticed the two little girls whispering with one another. Then the girls got up out of their seats and sat between the boys. After a minute Ryan, showing his independence, moved to a seat in the row behind. It wasn't long before his sister, Julie, slipped into the seat next to him and put her arm around him, not wanting him to feel rejected even though she had corrected his behavior. She knew instinctively how important it was to "[show] forth afterwards an increase of love" (D&C 121:43) after reproving. She wanted him to know she loved him even though she didn't approve of what he did.

Five-year-old Ulrike was not able to do that quite as easily. One day, when her father asked her why she looked so unhappy, she confided that she didn't like going to kindergarten. It turned out that a larger girl at school frequently pushed and kicked her.

Her father took this opportune moment to explain about loving our enemies. He challenged his little girl to answer each unkind deed with two kind deeds. That way she and her good deeds would always be victorious, because the kindness would outweigh the unkindness. They prayed together and her father was certain his daughter had learned a masterful lesson.

In a few days the father noticed that Ulrike's demeanor had improved, so he asked about the problem they'd discussed.

"Oh, she doesn't come to kindergarten anymore. My prayer was answered."

"And did you try the two kind deeds for each unkindness?"

"Yes. Once when she kicked me, I gave her two candies." Then, with a triumphant sparkle in her eyes, Ulrike added, "So her teeth will rot!"

It's hard, even for a child, to love someone who isn't being nice. It seems to be especially difficult for us as adults to show love unconditionally. Our children disobey us. They make choices that cause them—and us—grief. Our neighbors, our co-workers, and our church associates don't always agree with us. Sometimes people offend and even conspire against us. Granted, that's not nice. However, we need to leave the judging and sentencing to civil or Church authorities or to the Lord. Of us it is required to love unconditionally.

Unconditional love is one of the most lacking characteristics in human society. The absence of love leads to riots and wars, family instability, abuse, and court actions. Yet even in this wicked world there are some who understand unconditional love and live their lives accordingly.

My grandfather had a favorite saying that relates to this: "Be noble, and the nobleness in others, sleeping, but never dead, will rise in majesty to meet thine own." (James Russell Lowell.) I think that attitude has its roots in unconditional love. It is terrifically motivating to me.

Two men, business partners, separated over a disagreement on business practices. There were some rather hard feelings between them. Yet when one of these men was called to a leadership position in the ward in which they both resided, he asked for his former partner as a counselor. I believe this approaches the love the Savior wants us to exhibit.

Another man perceived he had been wronged by a neighbor. He harbored unkind feelings, said hurtful things about the neighbor, and refused to associate with him or even to speak civilly to him. The neighbor tried to discover the cause for the hard feelings, sorrowed at the rift in the friendship. However, he recognized that the other man had experienced difficult times, had undergone some stress, and may not have been seeing events in their true perspective. This neighbor made allowances in his heart for the extenuating circumstances that may have caused the feelings. He refused to say unkind things and continued to pray that the friendship could be resumed.

I believe that one of the reasons children are able to love so freely is because they assume that other people love everybody, too. To become as little children, maybe we who have been in the world longer should assume that everyone wants to do the best he or she can. If people don't succeed, maybe it's because they don't know what to do or how to do it. Maybe we could assume that although we're all different, we also all have a lot in common. We all want and need security, love, acceptance, and self-esteem. While we have to be discerning enough to avoid being deceived, we can still love everybody unconditionally. I think the Savior would like that.

These words of a Primary song verify that assumption, and express what we need to do to be loving, as children are:

If you don't walk as most people do,
Some people walk away from you,
But I won't! I won't!
If you don't talk as most people do,
Some people talk and laugh at you,
But I won't! I won't!
I'll walk with you. I'll talk with you.
That's how I'll show my love for you.
Jesus walked away from none.
He gave his love to ev'ryone.
So I will! I will!
Jesus blessed all he could see,
Then turned and said, "Come, follow me."
And I will! I will!
I will! I will!
I'll walk with you. I'll talk with you.
That's how I'll show my love for you.

A Child Is Loving

(Carol Lynn Pearson, "I'll Walk With You," *Children's Songbook* [Salt Lake City: The Church of Jesus Christ of Latter-day Saints, 1989], pp. 140–41.)

Chapter Five

A CHILD IS KIND

"Let all bitterness, and wrath, and anger,
and clamour, and evil speaking, be put away from you,
with all malice: And be ye kind to one another,
tenderhearted, forgiving one another,
even as God for Christ's sake hath forgiven you."
(Ephesians 4:31–32.)

One day Joseph, eight years old, was at school playing basketball and saw someone who was being left out of the game. "I went over and sat down and talked to him," said Joseph. I asked the others if he could play. They said, 'No!' This boy told me he didn't mind, but I could tell he wanted to be 'in.' I felt so bad all day that when I got home, I called him and told him to come over. We had lots of fun. It made him and me feel better."

I often hear the comment, "Children can be so unkind to one another." That is true. However, I maintain that unkind behavior is learned, and results from unmet needs of children as well as from poor examples. I believe that when children come into the world, their natural inclination is to be kind. When I see three-year-old Marie climb up on the bed by her one-year-old brother and sing and coo to him so that he will stop crying and fall asleep, I cannot help but think that that is a natural inclination.

Kindness can include generosity, benevolence, cordiality, and gentleness. A kind person is sympathetic, friendly, gentle, tender-hearted. When three-year-old Susan gets gum balls out of the machine and then says, "Mom, let's get some more for Jane Anne" (her older sister who is in kindergarten), that is kindness.

One late summer day as I was standing at the sink peeling carrots for dinner, the doorbell rang. I opened the door to discover eight-year-old Rebecca. Her bike was neatly parked on our front walk with the kickstand down. I expressed my delight in seeing her.

"I came to visit," she said as she seated herself primly on the sofa and crossed her legs. "I thought maybe you were missing children and would like to have a child come and visit you."

Rebecca cannot know how her kindness warmed my heart. It was true. Our grown children have been gone for several years, and I do miss the daily ring of children's laughter within the walls of our home. I really enjoyed our lovely, very grown-up visit together.

A Child Is Kind

The other day three-year-old Ben appeared at our front door clutching a precious little drooping dandelion. He couldn't bring himself to say a word, but a wide grin lighted his face as he thrust his hand forward for me to take the dandelion. Then, without a word, he bounded down the steps, across the lawn, and back to his home. I stood there warmed by his obvious joy in so kindly sharing with me.

It was fast Sunday. My husband bore his testimony, commenting that he was alone that day due to my being away on a Church assignment. As he concluded his testimony and sat down, eight-year-old Torri, the youngest daughter in a family of six children, bounced out of her seat and slipped into the row where Leonard was sitting. She sat down next to him, put both arms around his waist, gave him a big hug, then sat there cuddled next to him with his arm around her. She whispered, "I didn't want you to be alone." Kindness is one building block of service, and it can start young.

Two little girls were in Primary opening exercises when an announcement was made reminding teachers of the ward adult Valentine party. The leader making the announcement specifically addressed the girls' teacher, a young, single, recently returned missionary. He was encouraged to get a date and attend. The young man commented that he probably would not attend because he didn't think he could get a date.

The two little girls, much concerned for their teacher, decided to do something about his dateless situation. They went to his home when he wasn't there and got a picture of him from his family. They glued it to a poster on which they wrote, "Will you go out with me?" Then they took it to a young adult ward in the area, stood in the foyer with a clipboard and pencil, and stopped likely looking girls. In a few minutes they had several names. When they took the poster and list back to their teacher's house, he was mortified! But the girls, insistent, pointed out the names of the young adult women they thought had the most potential. Their teacher went to the Valentine party with a date recruited by his Primary girls!

Adam was feeling very kind when he tried to help his grandmother. Adam's grandmother told how this precocious seven-year-old sat looking at her most intently as she was visiting with other members of the family. Finally she looked at him and saw that he was scrutinizing her face. Then he said, "Grandmother, your face really has quite a few wrinkles, doesn't it?"

Grandmother smiled and replied, "Yes, it really does."

Adam said, "Well, let me tell you what I do. First I fill the sink up with water, and then I go like this." He pantomimed splashing water on his face. "Then I go like this," he said, pretending to splash his face again. "Then I go like this." A third time he splashed imaginary water on another part of his face. "Then I take the towel . . ." and he pretended to very gently pat his face all over. Then Adam looked up at his grandmother, beamed a big smile, and said, pointing to his cheek, "Just look, no wrinkles!"

Children have a seemingly innate desire to please others, to make things better, to "fix" a situation. Adam did. I suspect he got it from his father, Kelly.

It was a bitter cold winter in southeast Idaho and eleven-year-old Kelly had barely had time to arrive at school when he telephoned his mother.

"Mom, could you bring my old coat to school, please?" he asked.

"Why, Kelly?"

"Because I gave my new one away."

His mother tried to remain calm. "You *what?*"

"Mom, one of the Indian boys from the reservation came this morning with no coat on, and Mom, his ears were frost-bitten, and he was crying." The temperatures had been below zero. "Mom, he stood and waited for the bus for half an hour. I gave him my hat and my gloves too. I hope you don't mind. I knew I still had my old ones."

Kelly's ability to love has continued into his adulthood. He and his wife, natural parents of four, have adopted two babies from cultures different from theirs. Their motivation, besides a love of children, was to rescue the children from poverty and deprivation.

There are other adults like Kelly. At the entrances to the parking structure at the Church offices, security officers are at their posts in all weather. On the coldest days they are cloaked, hatted, and mufflered. My friend Betty Jo Jepsen has been known to stop as she drives in and drop off a Thermos of hot apple juice as a spontaneous and benevolent act of kindness to these hardy souls.

Ed Okazaki was an example of kindness and service before his death. Weekends would often find him and his wife, Chieko, at a homeless shelter passing out fresh oranges, giving his coat to a shivering soul, rushing to buy paper plates when the supply got low, or simply listening to someone's tale of woe.

Ruth Wright, my friend and co-worker, has a keen sense of when I need kindness. Even in the rush of deadlines and tight schedules, she will ask about something that has worried me. Or she will simply give me a reinforcing squeeze and say, "Don't worry."

I am amazed at the kindness of my daughters. (Mothers are always amazed when their children turn out well!) When I'm away from home overnight on Church business, Sara and her husband, Dave, will always drop in to visit with Leonard. Susan is diligent about seeing that her friends and family have appropriate birthday or wedding celebrations. Jane Anne always speaks to me in the kindest words and ways. These may seem unimpressive, but they exemplify the kindness that brings simple pleasure or gentle comfort to others.

Wouldn't it be a wonderful thing if grown-ups, hardened

and cynical though we are, would more often follow the kind impulses of our hearts and spontaneously do kind things, as children often do? Recognizing others' accomplishments, making others comfortable, soothing others' fears, assisting those in need—and doing these things unprogrammed and unexpected—would help us be more childlike and more Christlike.

Chapter Six

A CHILD IS COURAGEOUS

"Be strong and of a good courage;
be not afraid, neither be thou dismayed:
for the Lord thy God is with thee."
(Joshua 1:9.)

leven-year-old Shane stood in testimony meeting and bore his testimony. At the conclusion he said, "Brother and sisters, I know the gospel is true, and when I grow up I want to be a missionary and tell everyone that the gospel is true so they can be happy. I pray for Cory [his older brother] that he will repent, that he will stop doing what he is doing wrong, and that he will prepare himself to be worthy to serve a mission."

Those of us in the congregation were in awe at Shane's courageous declaration. We wondered what would happen.

A year and a half later, at his missionary farewell, Cory said, "I have had several people ask me what made me decide to go on a mission. It's because a year and a half ago I was sitting in testimony meeting with my family, and I didn't take the sacrament. Shane noticed that, and when he bore his testimony, he challenged me to repent and prepare for a mission. I thought, if Shane wants to go on a mission and he's watching me as his example, I have to live up to what he expects of me. The courage of my little brother made me want to go on a mission and gave me the courage to change so I could."

We do not always think of children as being courageous. Young children who are out of their comfort zone will be fearful. But children who do show courage are *so* courageous and *so* bold it is sometimes startling—and usually inspiring. They challenge us to greater courage. Terminally ill children, for example, often seem to approach impending death with a peace and acceptance that many adults cannot muster. Others show courage in approaching the unknown or the frightening or simply the everyday challenges.

I was watching children enter the Primary room in a little branch in Peru. Usually, the children assigned to give the scripture, prayer, and short talks sit in front, but none came forward. Primary began and the president called a child from the group to read a scripture. She called another child forward to offer a prayer. I could see they hadn't been assigned beforehand. Then, after the children had sung and she had greeted them, I knew it was time for the talks to be given.

The president looked around the room. I thought, "Surely she is not going to call on children extemporaneously to give talks." But that's exactly what she did!

"Juan," she said, motioning to a boy who appeared to be about ten years old, "will you come forward and give one of our talks, and when he is finished, Maria, will you do the same." I held my breath to see what would happen. I thought, "These children will be frightened to death! They will never want to come back to church again!"

Well, little Juan came forward without any hesitation, his

dark, rosy face gleaming above an almost sparklingly clean white shirt and tie. He was carrying his scriptures under his arm. He flipped through the pages of his scriptures. His eyes came to rest on one page and he said, "One of my favorite scriptures is . . . " and he proceeded to read a passage of scripture. Then he said, "I think the Lord is trying to teach us . . . " and he explained the principle he believed was the theme of that scripture. I don't remember the scripture to which he referred. I didn't pay much attention to that because I was so taken with the process he was using. Then he said, "Therefore, I think that we should . . . " and he explained how he felt he and the other children could apply the principle taught in that passage of scripture. He closed by bearing his testimony of the principle and sat down.

Courageous! That young man, though he had not been previously assigned, was prepared. He knew the scriptures, he understood them, and he recognized the application of the principles taught in the scriptures. His courage came from his preparation, from his love of the Lord, and, I suspect, from his innocence. "If ye are prepared ye shall not fear." (D&C 38:30.) I wondered if my children could have done that. I wondered if *I* could have.

My cousin's five-year-old son, Andy, was assigned to give a

talk in Primary. His mother said, "Let's decide what you're going to say."

"Oh, it's all right," he responded. "I know what I'm going to say."

Mothers just aren't usually too comfortable with that, so in a day or two she tried again. He reassured her that he knew what he was going to say. So on Saturday his mother said, "Andrew, let's pretend you're at Primary and practice what you're going to say so you won't be nervous when it's your turn."

With a sigh he conceded. To please his mother he would practice. He said, as he held up his own Book of Mormon, "In our family, we read the Book of Mormon together every day. We take turns reading. When it's my turn, since I can't read yet, my daddy reads for me and then I tell what it's about.

"I've learned a lot reading the Book of Mormon. Nephi was a good example. I hope I can be a good example like Nephi.

"I think it's a good thing to read the Book of Mormon. Children should read it. We can all read the Book of Mormon."

Andy's mother knew then that he would be all right giving his talk.

When Andy gave the talk in Primary, his mother could see from his shaking little hands that he was frightened, but because he had had experience with the Book of Mormon, he had something to say. And he believed what he said—this gave him courage to say it.

Joseph Smith was hardly more than a child when he courageously proclaimed that God had again spoken to man. He had had an experience he could not deny. He knew the truth and he had something to say.

In the first epistle of John we read, "And we have known and believed the love that God hath to us. God is love; and he that dwelleth in love dwelleth in God, and God in him. Herein is our love made perfect, that we may have boldness in the day of judgment: because as he is, so are we in this world. There is no fear in love; but perfect love casteth out fear." (1 John 4:16–18.)

Because it is so easy for children to love God, the security of that love helps them to be fearless, as John taught. But the love that is so easy for them to give and receive does not come without their being exposed to it. It is necessary for someone to give them the experience, or they won't know the love of God and will not be likely to know the courage borne of that love.

A testimony of truth, combined with their love of the Lord and of their parents, enabled Helaman's two thousand stripling warriors to defend their families and their country with courage. Probably their parents didn't wait till they were teenagers to start preparing them. The battles our children face today require an inner strength borne of love and preparation and experience and testimony. Many of them have that courage.

Laurel Rohlfing recounted these stories of two courageous children: "Brian, a Latter-day Saint boy, attended a school run by another church. One day the children were being very noisy as the teacher tried to read from the Bible. She closed the Bible and said, 'No wonder there are no prophets on the earth today. You children are so naughty that you wouldn't listen to them anyway.' Brian had an important choice to make. He could remain silent, or he could tell his teacher what he believed. He gathered his courage, quietly raised his hand, and said, 'Teacher, there is a prophet on the earth today. He lives in Salt Lake City.' The teacher was very interested in this information and asked him to tell her more about his church.

"Melissa's parents are divorced. On the weekends that she spends with her father, she attends church with him. But when she stays with her mother, she is not allowed to go. Melissa was given a part in the Children's Sacrament Meeting Presentation, but the presentation was scheduled for a weekend when she would be staying with her mother. Melissa was disappointed, because she wanted to participate. She prayed every night that her mother would allow her to go to church. On the day of the presentation, Melissa found the courage to tell her mother how important going to church was to her and to ask her mother for permission to attend and participate in the presentation. Her mother said yes! When Melissa stood at the pulpit, tears ran down her face as she told of her gratitude to Heavenly Father for answering her prayers and giving her the courage to choose the right." (*Friend*, July 1991, pp. 12–13.) Now, I don't know about you, but those children make me want to "be of good courage, and do it." (Ezra 10:4.)

For thirty years my friend Phyllis cared for her husband, who was afflicted with debilitating Parkinson's disease. She must have been discouraged many times, but whenever I was with her, she positively glowed with an aura of happiness and contentment. During this time she reared five teenagers, served on the Primary general board, was ward Relief Society president, and served a stake mission. Her courage was a result of her spiritual preparation, her love for the Lord, and her devotion to her husband.

James, a friend who has not married, has faced the discouragement of feeling lonely, watching most of his friends marry, dealing with financial, health, and spiritual problems of his extended family, and experiencing disappointments in personal relationships and the faltering testimonies of friends. While others like him lose courage and faith, James, prepared with testimony and a love of the Lord, has courageously been able to master his circumstances and make an interesting and full life for himself.

We too can refuse to be daunted, as these children and my friends do. The world needs more courage. Maybe we can help it grow.

A Child Is Courageous

We need to have the innocence, the unconditional love, and the believing hearts of children. But humility and meekness do not preclude the exercise of courage. To fail to have and exercise the courage of our convictions would not be in keeping with the charge we have to stand for righteousness in all times and all places.

Sometimes courage takes the form of tenacity—the ability to hold on and face the unpleasant when it is necessary, and to master personal weaknesses without giving up.

Sometimes courage involves seeking greater information or knowledge in order to better one's life or to improve the circumstances of another.

Sometimes courage means doing the right thing in the face of criticism, condemnation, and pain.

President Ezra Taft Benson, like all our prophets, set a great example of courage. He was often criticized for his policies when he was serving as Secretary of Agriculture during the Eisenhower administration. But he stood firm, saying, "I feel it is always good strategy to stand up for the right, even when it is unpopular. Perhaps I should say, especially when it is unpopular." (Sheri L. Dew, *Ezra Taft Benson, A Biography* [Salt Lake City, Deseret Book, 1987], p. 303.)

Right is often not popular. When we are courageous in unpopular circumstances, we are putting our trust in the Lord and caring more for the approval of our Heavenly Father and Savior than for the approbation of men. That is the kind of courage so many children possess. It is the kind we grown-ups need, to help us acquire the characteristics of the Savior.

Chapter Seven

A CHILD IS JOYFUL

"Men are, that they might have joy."
(2 Nephi 2:25.)

Three-year-old Mandy was at her grandmother's house on one of those October days that are cool and crisp on the edges and warm and soft in the middle. Grandmother's attention was diverted for a few moments and Mandy disappeared. When her grandmother found her, Mandy was standing outside with her little face turned upward toward the sun, and her eyes were closed. "Oh, Grandma, look!" she cried. "The sun is giving me a hug!"

One of the most delightful characteristics of children is their joyous approach to life. Nearly everything is wonderful or exciting or just plain fun to them.

For a number of years I have participated as part of the faculty at a Scout ranch where for two weeks each summer Church leaders learn about how Scouting is used in the Church. The families of stake leaders are marvelously taught and entertained all day while their parents are in training sessions. The children enjoy themselves and parents tell us how pleased they are that the children are so well cared for.

Once, after the second adventure-filled day, I watched one little boy of about six run up to his father. Breathlessly, almost unable to get the words out, he said, "Oh, Dad, Dad! It's ... it's ... it's just *too much fun!*"

Children have the capacity to enjoy life. Perhaps that's why

I love watching them play. Their enthusiasm and energy are stimulating and motivating to me. Usually, it does not take very much to entertain them. The simple things bring them the most joy—a little sand, a bucket of water, a big cardboard box, a few dress-ups, some sunshine, even a rainstorm.

When our youngest child, Sara, was seven years old, we moved to a new home framed on all sides by fields of sagebrush. As spring approached, the sunshine and the rain brought a green haze to the earth beneath the sagebrush. This provided a most intriguing new experience for Sara. As she looked at that green grass and the sagebrush, she could imagine a playhouse. So, armed with stuffed animals and blankets, she created in the field south of our home a most wonderful adventure—a house in the sunshine. It had a kitchen, a bedroom, a living room, a playroom. She opted to spend solitary time, hours of it, in happy, creative play there. From time to time she shared the pretending with a friend, but for the most part it was her own private experience.

The first Christmas after Leonard and I were married we went to my parents' home on Christmas Eve. My younger brother Norris, who was two years old at the time, was really excited about Christmas. Mother said, "He has loved the tree, and we've bought him some presents, but I don't know that he'll have something tomorrow that will keep him occupied as long as the toys his older brothers will be getting."

Well, for Leonard, a designer and artist, that was an opportunity to exercise his creativity. Mother had just bought a new washer, and the cardboard box it had come in was still in the shed. It would make a wonderful little playhouse. We went to the grocery store for another box, which we took apart to make a side room and a roof. We found some powdered tempera paints and Leonard created a darling miniature Swiss chalet like those in his native Switzerland.

Two-year-old Norris was delighted. The windows and doors opened. The box was just the right size for him to crawl in with a blanket and a pillow. It was a huge success and it didn't cost us anything more than our time, imagination, and materials we already had on hand. It lasted until Norris was too big to fit inside anymore.

This project was so successful that when our own children starting coming we made a "playbox" for them too. It lasted for years. It got left in the sunshine and the paint faded. A corner of it got in the sprinkler and warped a little. But it continued to be used until one day it was left in the rain and it literally fell apart. And when it did the children mourned.

The simplicity of what brings children joy is almost *too*

easy: a pan lid and a spoon to bang on it with, a bowl of uncooked macaroni and a paper cup, a conversation in the dark, the face of a pansy, a squirrel to feed, or a woodpecker drilling a tree. Could joy be that easy for grown-ups?

The basic elements of the world are the most intriguing to a child—the delight of soap bubbles, lying on your back on the grass with your sister sprinkling pieces of grass on your face to see how long you can keep from laughing, rolling sideways down a grassy hill, exploring sand dunes, beaches, oceans, streams.

A Child Is Joyful

I believe children need a childhood. I believe they need to be able to find out for themselves what the world is all about. And that is really what they want to do. To children, play is their work. Play teaches them who they are and what they are supposed to do in life. As they play, they develop relationships with others and learn what they are capable of. They need some unstructured time to play, to learn on their own and at their own pace.

When I was seven years old the Church celebrated the centennial of the pioneers' entrance into the Salt Lake Valley. We came from Seattle, where we were living at the time, to be part of the celebration. I know there was a magnificent parade, but I don't remember it. I know there were crowds of people.

There were probably ice cream cones and lemonade. But what I remember, and that most vividly, is the balloon. The helium balloon, my first. I will never forget how it smelled, how it felt, how huge it was. They said to be careful or it would fly away, and they tied it to my wrist with a string. It was a breathtaking experience for me. Because I have been to many parades since then, I know there must have been gorgeous floats, rousing bands, and lots of noise. What I remember is standing on the northeast corner of South Temple and Main Street with that first helium balloon.

While I believe children should be allowed to have a childhood, I also believe it is important for grown-ups to run through the grass barefoot and to walk in mud puddles once in a while. I need every now and then to giggle over the tickle of a ladybug on the back of my leg, and to imagine animals in the clouds. I believe that if we can enjoy the simple pleasures of life as adults, we can be more appreciative of our Heavenly Father and his creations and the gifts he has given us. I think it increases our spiritual sensitivities. In fact, I believe that the more well developed we are spiritually, the more joy we find in simple pleasures. We don't have the driving need for more and more sensory stimulation that traps many in enslaving habits.

During periods of extended training for our Primary general board members, we take frequent breaks. Activities during those breaks have included making giant soap bubbles, having a jacks tournament, roller blading, flying kites, and presenting silly skits. It seems an appropriate way for Primary ladies to relax! Also it helps us appreciate the children we serve.

At a recent family reunion, I learned something new about my seventy-six-year-old father. He is a great jacks player! We laughed as we both had to pad our joints with towels to sit on the kitchen floor for the game. My father and I are close. But if we weren't, I can see how playing together could mend hearts and open communication. It is rejuvenating to our souls to play as little children.

Children are joyful because they look on the bright side of things. Jacqueline said, "Grandma died. Well, it's just for a little while, isn't it?"

Two-year-old Annie was dressing one morning with the help of her mother. Suddenly Annie looked worried and said, "I lost." Her mother was puzzled. Annie looked anxiously about the room, then ran to stand in front of a large mirror. Relieved, she said with a sigh, "Here I am."

Sue's three-year-old grandson, Trent, was visiting. As they were playing outside, he started stomping on some potato bugs. Sue called him to her and explained about reverence for life.

"Those potato bugs were some potato bug's children," she said, "or some bug's mother and dad or grandma and grandpa." She explained that the other bugs would miss them if Trent kept stamping on them and killing them. He looked very solemnly at her and listened carefully. She thought she had solved the problem, teaching him a most significant lesson. The next time she turned around she saw him stomping even more vigorously on potato bugs. Sue was dismayed and said, "Trent, I thought we had a talk about that."

Trent said, "It's okay, Grandma, because I'm going to get them all and then all the families can be together forever in heaven."

Andy's mother asked her five-year-old to explain a little drawing he had made. He tried several times to get the right words out to explain and then he looked up at her with a big sigh and said, "Well, it's in my head even if it isn't in yours."

The spontaneity of children is part of what helps them experience joy. Andy and his father were outside washing off the sidewalk when Andy took the hose and squirted his dad. When Andy's back was turned, his dad got the hose and squirted Andy. They laughed and giggled as they played together in the water. Finally, when his dad was standing near the pool, Andy ran and pushed him. Dad took a great leap into the pool, making Andy feel that he had really pushed hard. Andy squealed in delight. He bounced into the house with all the enthusiasm of a four-year-old and exclaimed to his mother, "Oh, Mother, we had the most fun! And you know, we didn't even plan it. It was *spontaneous* fun. This is the most fun Friday I have had because it was spontaneous. Next Friday let's do exactly the same thing and have spontaneous fun again!" He revelled in the word *spontaneous*, even if he didn't understand completely what it meant.

A Child Is Joyful

Life is serious, difficult, and fraught with disappointments. It's easy to lose the joyous sparkle of childhood, to become cynical and morose. But if we are to become as children, should not the joys of living be evident in what we do and how we behave?

One of my fond childhood memories is of my father arriving home from the office or church meetings. As he entered the door he would burst into song, double forte. He woke us up in the morning that way too, but pianissimo (that is, if the meadowlarks had not already done the job for him). What a memory for a child!

We grown-ups often underestimate the joy a child can feel learning principles of the gospel. Our granddaughter Marie was not yet three when the phone rang on my desk at the office one day. On the phone was her little voice saying, "Grandma G, I went to Primary."

"Oh, what did you do?"

"We had a story."

"What was the story?"

"A man couldn't see. Jesus put mud on his eyes and when he washed it off, he could see!"

Clearly she was thrilled with what she had learned. She marvelled at the miracle. She marvelled at the power of the Savior. She marvelled at the simplicity of the cure.

While stories and games are important tools we can use to help teach children gospel principles, they must be focused on a purpose. A mother reported that her nine-year-old son said he really liked his Primary teacher, who was a former bishop, high councilor, and stake president's counselor. The mother asked, "What is it you like so much about him?"

"Well, you know how most teachers just tell you stories and play games with you," came the reply. "He teaches us important things, things we really need to know." Our children find joy in learning new, important things.

Six-year-old Marie lay on the bed next to me while I was telling her stories from the Old Testament. Marie had had a fun-filled, busy, and exhausting day of play at our house. She could hardly keep her eyes open, yet she continued to ask for more of the Old Testament stories. She stopped me frequently, asking for clarification on points of the story. Though her eyelids were very heavy, she denied being sleepy. Her desire to know more about spiritual things was almost insatiable. I could stop only when Marie had finally succumbed to sleep.

A number of years ago, when President Spencer W. Kimball called me to serve as a counselor in the Primary general presidency, I asked him if he had any counsel for me. He looked at me seriously and said, "Yes, I would counsel you to find joy in serving the Lord." I have given much thought to that counsel, and I have come to realize that missing the joy in Church service and in life in general is missing half the experience. I know that our Father in heaven has given us this earth and this life and the fullness of the gospel in order that we might find eternal joy. Some of that joy can be experienced here and now. And maybe finding joy in simple pleasures—including the beautifully simple principles of the gospel—can make us more as little children.

Chapter Eight

WHAT WE CAN DO FOR CHILDREN

"He commanded that their little ones should be brought. . . .
And [he] said unto them: Behold your little ones."
(3 Nephi 17:11, 23.)

A bishop told me about extending a call to a woman in his ward. Together they read from the Book of Mormon, Third Nephi, chapter 17.

They read how the Savior invited the Nephites to bring their children to him, how Jesus prayed for the children and blessed them, and how angels appeared and ministered to them within the fire that encircled them. Those familiar words are powerful, poetic verses.

Then the bishop said, "Sister Breinholt, the Savior cannot personally be in our ward every Sunday. But through inspiration from our Heavenly Father, we are calling you to do for some children in our ward what the Savior would do for them if he were here. We are calling you to serve as a Primary teacher!"

When I heard that extraordinary experience, I wanted to study those verses again to understand better what the Savior did with the Nephite children, and what he would do for our children if he were here. I spent considerable time reading and contemplating those verses. My thoughts took many turns that were new adventures for me.

For example, the Savior's invitation was neither casual nor inconsequential. "He *commanded* that their little ones should be brought." (Verse 11; italics added.) Also notice what verse eleven doesn't say. It doesn't say, Never mind the little ones because they aren't accountable yet. It doesn't indicate that the children were to be taken elsewhere so they wouldn't disrupt the proceedings. It doesn't imply that the children would not understand. But it *does* teach that children need to learn the significant things of the kingdom. God's little children share with all of us a divine right to spiritual enlightenment.

Verse 12: "So they brought their little children and set them down upon the ground round about him, and Jesus stood in the midst." I thought of the struggle some members have with pride that keeps them from being willing to serve in Primary. Too many consider serving children to be beneath them. Clearly the Savior felt that the Nephite children were not only worthy to be in his presence, but also worthy of his time and attention. The children needed him, and he stood right in their midst. Surely, if the Savior considers the children worthy of his presence, time, and attention, we should be willing to offer these gifts too.

Verse 12 also indicates that Jesus waited "till they had all been brought unto him." He wasn't looking for a representative sample, and he wasn't content with just some of the children. He wanted them all to be there, and he ministered to them all, regardless of differences or challenges that might cause some of us to neglect, abuse, or avoid some children.

Then Jesus prayed unto the Father so powerfully that "no tongue can speak, neither can there be written by any man, neither can the hearts of men conceive so great and marvelous things." (Verse 17.) And the children were there! They heard that prayer; they saw this event; and, as we read later, they were affected by it. Children can understand and should witness marvelous events—priesthood blessings, special ward and family fasts, the testimonies and prayers of their parents and leaders, and gospel discussions with people they love.

"He took their little children, one by one, and blessed them, and prayed unto the Father for them." (Verse 21.) Jesus was ministering to a group of about 2,500 men, women, and children. Consider how much time it must have taken for him to bless and pray over each child, "one by one." He must have held many of them in his arms or on his lap. And he wept because he was overcome with joy.

"He spake unto the multitude, and said unto them: Behold your little ones." (Verse 23.) Jesus specifically directed the attention of the multitude to the children. To me, the word *behold* is significant. It implies more than just "look and see." When the Lord instructed the Nephites to *behold* their little ones, I believe he was telling them to give attention to their children, to contemplate them, to look beyond the present and see their eternal possibilities.

"As they looked to behold . . . they saw the heavens open, and they saw angels descending out of heaven as it were in the midst of fire; and they came down and encircled those little ones about, and they were encircled about with fire; and the angels did minister unto them." (Verse 24.)

I can't help but wonder what would have happened if the multitude had just looked and not *beheld* with spiritual eyes. Would they have seen the angels descend? Could they have watched their children encircled about with fire? Would they have been able to observe as the angels ministered to their children? It is significant that later, the Savior gave the most sacred teachings to the children, then loosed their tongues so they could teach the multitude. (See 3 Nephi 26:14.)

Is it any wonder that, following the Savior's visit, the Nephites lived in peace and righteousness for two hundred years? That's a long time! That's about the age of the United States. Imagine! Principles were passed on for that long.

Let us not underestimate the capacity and potential power of today's children to perpetuate righteousness. No group of people in the Church is as receptive to the truth, both in efficiency of learning and in degree of retention. No group is as vulnerable to erroneous teaching, and no group suffers more from neglect and abuse. Children cannot protect or provide for themselves. We, the adults of the world, must open the way for them. Our little children worldwide deserve to be "remembered and nourished by the good word of God, to keep them in the right way." (Moroni 6:4.)

Jesus gave us a clear pattern to follow in fulfilling our responsibility to nurture and teach children. Our challenges differ from those of the Nephites because we live in a different time. But the Savior's way is timeless. In his church, there can be no other way.

And what is his way? As he demonstrated, our physical presence and attention are vital to children in our families, church, and communities. We can know their needs and minister to them when we spend time with them. We can behold our children in their eternal perspective and see that they all know of the Savior and learn the significant truths of his gospel. We can help them witness marvelous spiritual events. They can hear our earnest prayers in their behalf. And we can be their ministering angels on earth if we follow the Lord's example.

Gratitude fills me when I hear of those who respond to

children in Christlike ways. I read of a bishop's counselor who noticed a little boy sitting on the floor crying one busy Sunday. Disregarding his own busy schedule, this good man immediately focused his attention on the weeping child. He sat right down on the floor and held the little boy close until the crying subsided and the boy was able to explain what was wrong. People had to step around them for nearly ten minutes. Then, comforted, the child went off down the hall holding the hand of this earthly ministering angel. That bishop's counselor probably responded naturally, as he would have to his own child.

I sense that the Savior would have done that too.

Children need to be appreciated for what they are today, and they need us to do what we can to make their lives better today. It is not enough to say we must care for them because of what they will be in the future, although that is true and important. They need today to be wonderful too. We can respond in many ways to children in physical, emotional, or spiritual need.

A young Latter-day Saint mother from Alaska, living in Russia temporarily, visited the home of a member family with two small sons. She learned that the children read and loved the scriptures and hungered to know more. Then she attended the small branch and found that because the Church was so new there, they had no experience in teaching the children on Sunday. The members asked for her help.

She said, "Knowing what the children were missing, I had an overwhelming feeling I should help them." Then she added, "I felt I would be held accountable if I did not." Responding to the requests of the Russian members, she helped them organize a Primary. She taught them how to teach their children through lessons and songs. She was a ministering angel to these children by helping the adults learn how to teach them in the organized church.

A friend of mine received an invitation to the temple wedding of a young man she had taught in Primary. When she responded to the invitation, she asked, "David, you moved away, and I haven't seen you for years. Why did you think of me?"

"Sister McMullin," he answered, "you taught us about scrubbing our hands and wearing clean clothes when we would pass the sacrament. You taught us about being clean inside, too. When I was faced with temptations and decisions in my dating years, your voice would come into my mind: 'A deacon is clean inside and out.' I am worthy to go to the temple because of you. That's why I want you to come with us." She did not know until then that she had been a ministering angel to that boy. Sometimes we never know. But following the Savior's pattern makes us instruments to provide what the Lord would provide if he were here.

A sister missionary in New Guinea with her husband wrote us of teaching little children the gospel under a tree at a large coconut plantation. They tell scripture stories and sing songs. The children are excited to hear and participate, and are most attentive. They happily anticipate the monthly visits of the missionaries. After the lessons, the children line up for drinks of scarce and precious cool water from a plastic jug that these earthly ministering angels fill and freeze before they come. By simply accepting the challenge of serving a mission, this wonderful couple find they are earthly ministering angels to children.

I sense that the Savior would approve.

Each of us, whatever our circumstances, can help a child in a particular, important way that no one else can. We can give that child life-giving water, food, love, comfort, and protection. And we can offer the "living water" of the gospel.

As we minister to children with the same devotion and commitment demonstrated by the Savior, we bless them with testimony and the courage to resist evil. These are effective preventive measures that can help children in many ways. We can rescue them from abuse. We can help them know joy. We can strengthen them spiritually. We can help stem the raging tide of today's epidemic of immorality. The gospel can, and must, become a way of life for children today. Imagine what their lives can be like and what tomorrow's Church could be like if we fulfill the needs of our children today! Imagine what will happen if we don't.

By ministering to children we, like the Nephites, can help the gospel live for many generations. When we see their pure character, it validates our paying attention to them, being with them, and teaching them. There is no doubt that we must capitalize on their receptivity, their humility, their ability to learn, and put into their environment those things that will allow them to reach full flower. For in our hands are our most valuable and our most vulnerable resource—our children.

The innocence of children before the age of accountability sometimes makes us feel that it's not necessary to worry about them. Church leaders and parents sometimes rationalize that because children are not accountable until age eight, it is not necessary to focus on their spiritual needs. Nothing could be more wrong. Such shortsightedness could result in negative eternal consequences. Children do not live in a bubble. Even though Satan may be unable to tempt little children before baptism, we who have contact with them can let them get into habits or cause them to behave in ways that will lead them to sin when they do become accountable. Our families, our society, our church are only as solid or virtuous as today's generation of children. As Jeffrey Holland put it in a BYU Education Week speech in 1981, "As a Church we are just one generation away from extinction. All we would have to do is not teach the children for one generation."

Our generation will be held accountable for what we do or do not teach our children. The Lord chastised Frederick G. Williams, saying, "You have not taught your children light and truth, according to the commandments; and that wicked one hath power, as yet, over you, and this is the cause of your affliction." (D&C 93:42.)

It is easy for us to think that our children are all right. The innocence of young children can be deceptive, lulling us into a false sense of security regarding their spiritual development. But the fires that often don't start to rage until the teenage years may have been kindled in that innocent childhood.

The responsibility to teach children in their innocence was articulately described by Elder H. Verlan Andersen in his conference talk of October 1991:

"How will it be possible during the Millennium for the

people to remain righteous for almost a thousand years? . . . I believe that [the answer] consists in this: Parents teaching their children the gospel, and doing so especially during that early period of their lives when they cannot be tempted.

"Evidence that this was so among the Nephites and Lamanites is found in a miracle the Lord performed with respect to their little children. He separated the children from their parents, taught them greater things than he had taught the multitude, and then the children taught these greater things to their fathers. (See 3 Nephi 26:14–16.) Does not this event help us to understand the miraculous change in that society?

"Let us assume that the Lord, after having demonstrated the superior spiritual capabilities of children, instructed the parents to follow his example and that they did so. Would not the children, having been taught properly, have continued to live righteously after reaching maturity; and in the process of training them, would not the parents have become equally humble and righteous? How, otherwise, can we explain this astounding historical event?

"With respect to the Millennium, the Lord has given this information regarding the parents who will live in that society:

" 'And the earth shall be given unto them for an inheritance; and they shall multiply and wax strong, and their children shall grow up without sin unto salvation.' (D&C 45:58.)

"Obviously, the parents who will inherit the earth will be those who have learned to raise their children without sin unto salvation." (*Ensign,* November 1991, p. 80.)

Elder Marion G. Romney gave this wise counsel: "By the exercise of patience, long-suffering, and love, the good will and confidence of our children must be won. Time and understanding must be devoted to teaching and training them so that they *voluntarily* comply with the revealed truths of the gospel." (*Relief Society Magazine,* March 1964, pp. 167–68; italics added.)

What We Can Do for Children

Chapter Nine

CHILDREN AT PEACE

"All thy children shall be taught of the Lord;
and great shall be the peace of thy children."
(3 Nephi 22:13.)

Seven-year-old Jamie loved her mother dearly. The family had known for nearly a year that their wife and mother was dying of cancer. The father and seven children fasted, and prayed; they pleaded with the Lord to heal her. Everything possible was done for their mother, yet at the end of three painfully difficult months, she passed from this life.

In the first hours following her death, the father brought the grieving family together for prayer. After prayer, the children went to their separate rooms to prepare for bed. Jamie, who had spent many hours with her mother and was devoted to her, knelt at her own bedside. "Heavenly Father," she prayed through her tears, "we thank thee for the great mom you gave us. We thank thee for helping us try to make her well. Help us to be good so we can live with her again." Without a hint of bitterness, this little girl continued for several minutes in a sweet attitude of peaceful prayer, reflecting her understanding and acceptance of her mother's death.

Jamie was a child at peace. How did she come to that peace? She had been prepared by parents with spiritual understanding.

Our children—precious children of our Heavenly Father throughout the earth—are among the most valiant spirits to come into the world. We have a sacred responsibility to bestow on them a legacy of peace.

Our Heavenly Father has promised peace to his children. "All thy children shall be taught of the Lord; and great shall be the peace of thy children." (3 Nephi 22:13.) Peace in the Lord can give them freedom from self-doubt, freedom from fear, freedom from the confinement of their environment, freedom from enslaving habits. His peace can free them to unfold from the tender buds they are into mature and fruitful adults.

Just as the fragile bud contains all of the essential elements to develop into a lovely plant or flower, so does each child come to us with the potential for individual self-fulfillment of his or her eternal destiny. For both flowers and children, in order for what is inside to be fully developed, they must be nurtured from the outside. Plants require light, water, air, and nutrients to thrive. The human spirit thrives on love, knowledge of its origin, and teachings of a spiritual nature. We must provide a favorable environment for spiritual growth and the peace that will accompany it. This peace I speak of will result in quiet assurances even in the midst of worldly pressures and turmoil.

This simple, charming experience exemplifies the peace that can come when a child knows a direction to take. Seven-year-old Susan was approaching her eighth birthday and baptism. She and her sisters were playing outside in the yard. When she came in to get a drink of water, I said to her, "Honey, it's time for dinner, will you call your sisters?" So she went to the door and called out to them to come in the house because it was time for dinner. They didn't want to come, so they said, "Oh, it isn't time. We don't want to come in. You are just fooling us!" and they accused her of not telling the truth.

Well, Susan pulled herself up in all of her seven-year-old dignity, put her hands on her hips and said, "It is *too* dinner time, and you can believe me because I'm going to be baptized, and I tell the truth!" Susan had a strong commitment to be repentant and to do right. She wanted her sisters to know they could depend on her to tell them the truth. Her understanding brought her the peace necessary to defend her actions. Such conviction and determination would serve anyone well.

The children need our help. They need us to give them knowledge and understanding. They need us to help them obtain the peace of the Lord. Today is neither too early nor too late to prepare the children, and anyone can do it. A new family just beginning, an established family with children of several ages, a family with one parent, grandparents, aunts and uncles, neighbors, and kind, understanding Church leaders and teachers—all of us can teach children of the Lord.

We begin by teaching what we are. The children need to see in us what they can become. They need to see us keeping the commandments. We must come unto the Lord and seek for the peace of the gospel in our own lives. "Learn of me," he said, "and listen to my words; walk in the meekness of my Spirit, and you shall have peace in me." (D&C 19:23.) When we are at peace, then our children can be at peace.

A wise bishop once told me: "I have seen families where parents are at home with the gospel, where gospel principles are a matter-of-fact, everyday way of life, where parents treat their children with courtesy and respect with the full understanding that they are children of God. In these homes, the children seem to be at peace because their parents have given them a clear message. They know they are children of God. They feel their worth and have focus to their lives, knowing that eternity is their goal."

To some, a family such as the ones that bishop described may seem impossible to attain. No family is perfect—all are made up of human beings with mortal weaknesses who sometimes go astray. But family members, including parents, can begin where they are and learn and grow together.

We have been promised that family home evening, family prayer, and family scripture reading can strengthen and give direction to each member and can knit the family together. If you haven't been having family home evening or family prayer, you may feel awkward about beginning. That's all right. Do it anyway. Gather the family together, tell them that although you haven't been doing so, you want to begin to unitedly ask for the blessings of our Heavenly Father. Now, I must warn you that Satan will attempt to thwart your efforts, because family strength is a threat to his work. So persevere, even though it takes some effort and planning to overcome negative attitudes and obstacles.

When the family gathers for evening prayer, it is a good time for sharing the day's experiences, reading the scriptures, and bearing testimonies. Children especially need to hear the testimonies of their parents. One family repeats an Article of Faith every evening for a week, or memorizes a scripture, or recites the names of the books in the Book of Mormon. I visited in a home where sit-ups follow morning prayer and push-ups are the ritual after evening prayer. True principles are taught in this experience, too. Another family focuses on one child or a parent each day, with each member telling something good about that person. It takes just a few minutes. Children of all ages need to hear positive observations about themselves—especially from their parents.

Immerse the children in the stories of Jesus so they can know him and imagine what it must have been like to have lived when he was on the earth. Tell them how he took the children on his knee and blessed them and prayed for them. Tell them how the people knew he was the Son of God. For example, when I was a child, I loved to hear about the Savior's triumphal entry into Jerusalem. Many people heard that Jesus was coming to Jerusalem for the Feast of the Passover. They had heard he was the Son of God. They went out to meet him. Imagine what it must have been like to be a child in that happy crowd. The scripture says it was "a very great multitude." (Matthew 21:8.) They were probably waiting along the narrow streets of Jerusalem, becoming more and more excited as they strained to see if he was coming yet.

Then, as he came into view, riding on a donkey, can't you just hear a great cheer going up? The people spread their clothes and tree branches on the ground for the donkey to walk on, like they did for kings, and they waved palm leaves in the air. They cried, "Hosanna to the Son of David . . . hosanna in the highest." (Matthew 21:9.) Oh, wouldn't you love to have been there?

Tell the children about the Savior so they will trust him,

develop a desire to be like him, and want to be with him again. Yes, our homes can provide peace for the children.

Primary children can read and discuss the Book of Mormon. A nine-year-old boy in Wisconsin spoke in the children's sacrament meeting presentation in his ward about something he had learned that brought him peace:

"When my father told our family we would be moving to Wisconsin, my mother reminded us of Lehi's family. Like them, I was leaving the only home I had known, all my friends, my school, my ward. Luckily *we* got to bring all our possessions with us though they were in storage for three months, and we missed having a house and our 'precious things.'

"My mother reminded us of how Nephi accepted this challenge—willingly—knowing that the Lord would 'prepare a way for them that they may accomplish the thing which he commanded them.'

"I have learned that I can do without things, but not without my family. My brothers, sister, and I have tried to be more like Nephi than his complaining brothers. I am grateful for the things that the Book of Mormon teaches us."

When children are taught of the Lord, we bestow on them a gift, a legacy of peace that can lead them to eternal life. We must not fail them.

Chapter Ten

BECOMING AS A LITTLE CHILD

"Verily I say unto you, Except ye be converted, and become as little children,
ye shall not enter into the kingdom of heaven."
(Matthew 18:3.)

B rother J. Kent Millington, who was serving as a high council advisor to Primary, wrote the following:

"A Primary leader held up two silver dollars. One was old and dull with accumulated dirt and grime. The other was a shiny new silver dollar. The old one was still very usable and had great value.

" 'If we rub the two together, an interesting thing happens,' he said. 'The old silver dollar will lose some of its grime and will be polished by the new one.

" 'That's what happens to adults who associate with children in Primary. We rub against shiny, newly minted souls. Not only are we polished, but they are further shined as they respond to the Spirit and to the gospel truths we teach them.'

"I love that analogy. We must expose as many adults as we can to children. Adults need the polishing effect that comes from working with beautiful little souls. They need to be exposed to the faithfulness, the love, the trust, and the hope that reside in the hearts and minds of little children.

"Sadly, however, instead of our becoming like little children, I'm afraid we spend too much time training them to become like us— sometimes despairing and distrustful; often seeking after unimportant or inappropriate things; occasionally insensitive and hateful. As adults, we must not overlook every opportunity to be cleaned off and polished up. . . .

"The shiny cleanliness of children can be preserved. And as we do our part in polishing them, we can be polished ourselves. This is our great blessing and opportunity." (*Ensign,* March 1986, p. 48.)

In order to become more like children, we need to take every opportunity to be with them. When we associate with children, we are able to see the qualities that make them Christ-like. Only when we are with them can we learn from them.

Some people avoid children. A friend who was released from serving in the Young Women organization of her ward was speculating on how she would now spend her time. I commented that she might have the blessing of finally being called to teach in Primary.

"Oh, no!" she declared. "Children are not my thing. I don't like them, and they don't like me. Teenagers I can understand and relate to, but children are a total mystery!"

If children are a model for our immortality, we need to seek experiences with them that give us opportunities to be polished and refined and have our souls softened.

Increasing exposure to children makes us secure and confident around them. I know a single woman who throws parties for the neighborhood children. Another single friend spends individual time with each niece and nephew, and also plans slumber parties including them all. Others volunteer at women's and children's shelters or in local child-advocacy organizations.

Some of the most enthusiastic proponents of children are men who teach in Primary. Former bishops, elders quorum presidents, high councilors, and stake presidents think Primary is the best-kept secret in the Church. They like the spontaneity of the children and the quality of the lessons. They are impressed with the capacity of today's children to comprehend the important concepts of the gospel. They often find themselves simply enjoying the children.

When my husband, Leonard, was bishop, the Primary nursery leader told me one day how wonderful she thought it was that he came into the nursery frequently. I was surprised because he had not told me about doing so. She said, "Oh, yes! He just comes through the door and the children run to him and reach with outstretched arms for him to pick them up."

When I told Leonard about my conversation, he said, "Of course I go in the nursery. In there, everybody loves me. Wouldn't you want to go where everybody loves you?"

A friend who had served many years in responsible priesthood callings said, "I had no idea what I was missing! Why, in Primary I am teaching the gospel in the most clear and simple ways, and the children drink it all in. They hang on my every word. I feel the influence of the Holy Spirit during many of the lessons. Of all the callings I've had, this is my very favorite!"

As I continue to mature, I realize that at this empty-nest stage of my life, in order to be with children, I have to plan and structure experiences that put me in their presence. We had a neighborhood Christmas party at our house this year. We invited the children, much to the surprise of their parents. The happily noisy party was only about thirty minutes old when two mothers said to me quietly, "We vote next year not to have the children!" I could see that for these parents who work hard with and for their children every day, it may not have been as much fun to include the children as it was for me. I thanked them for being willing to bring their children so I could have my "kid fix."

As I've considered some qualities of children and how to acquire them in order to be "polished" and childlike and prepared to meet the Savior, I've concluded that we, like children, must be willingly submissive to all that the Lord may ask of us.

In the earliest stages of development, children tend to obey in order to avoid harm or punishment. As they mature, they begin to add to that motivation the desire to please those whom they regard highly—parents and leaders, for example. As they grow into older childhood and adulthood, they have the capacity to be motivated by their internalized values. They are able to do what they think is best, regardless of how others feel.

When sixteen-year-old Susan was working as a lifeguard at a water park, her supervisor scheduled her for a Sunday shift. She was concerned, and I said, "You can tell them your parents won't let you work on Sunday."

She responded, "No, I don't want to work on Sunday because *I* don't think it's right." When that kind of personal motivation is linked with love for Heavenly Father and Jesus and the desire to please them, we are functioning at our most mature spiritual level. Then it becomes easy to submit to the will of the Father, for our will is his will.

It is good for children to want to please their parents and leaders. It helps them understand and relate to pleasing their Heavenly Father. How can we help them also reach the level of consciously internalizing principles, taking them as their own and committing to those principles for a lifetime? We can give them the kind of reinforcement that helps them realize they *have* internalized the principle.

For example, often we will say to children, "Oh, you're a

good child. I'm so proud of you. You made me happy." That's good reinforcement, and they need that from us, but the higher motivation is for them to want to do good because *they* think it is best. A response to reinforce that sort of internal motivation might be, "Doesn't it feel good to behave that way?" or "Aren't you proud of yourself?" We need to do the same thing for ourselves, realizing that although we do some things to please others (including our Father in heaven), we also can find personal satisfaction in these pursuits.

To turn ourselves totally to the Lord requires such trust in Him! As I was growing up, I often thought I would like to have a report card from the Lord. Now I am inclined to think, no! I don't want to know what that report would say! This fear, of course, is based on my excruciating awareness of my insufficiencies. However, the Lord, knowing all that I know about myself, also knows much, much more. He knows all the circumstances that contribute to my being as I am. He also has the perspective of my possibilities. I know he must wish me to be better, yet he weeps with me in my discouragement and tempers his opinion of me with his omniscience and his love. And so I can trust to him my fears, my hopes, my weaknesses, and my pain. Because he knows more about me than I do, and loves me more than I can fathom, I am safe with him.

I watched five-year-old Tim sit on the side of the pool for three full sessions of swimming lessons. Others were splashing happily, but fear paralyzed him and nothing the teacher did could persuade him to venture into the water. Then his father came. Tim jumped into the pool to his father, over and over again. His trust in his dad enabled him to bridle his fear and he played, being supported and encouraged by one who knew Tim's capacity better than he did.

Such trust facilitates the submission to our Father's will that is required of us. Rather than tentatively putting a toe in, we can jump with full force, joyfully and willingly, into his waiting arms. We can put aside *childish* things and become true *childlike* Saints, even "children of Christ." (See Mosiah 5:7.)

As we submit "even as a child doth submit to his father" (Mosiah 3:19), we can accept callings that may seem beyond our capacity, knowing he will make us able. We can dismiss the judgments of others, knowing his is the only will to please. We can be more humble because our submission has stripped us of pride. We can become innocent because we follow the Savior's example. We can be kind because in a child of Christ there is no jealousy, malice, or unkindness. We can be tolerant of our own imperfections because, as four-year-old David told his father who accidentally knocked the popcorn off the table,

"It's okay, Dad. Life is life and sometimes you don't do good!" We can be joyful because He has taken away our sorrows, and we know this life is but a moment. In this childlike state, we will be more receptive to the Spirit than we have ever been before. Our knowledge and understanding will increase, helping us shed the childish, but enhancing the childlike. We will indeed be more ready to enter into the kingdom of heaven.